Sustain-Ability
How a corporate conscience helps
business sustain the ability to win

Sustain-Ability

How a corporate
conscience helps business
sustain the ability to win

Daniel W. Bena

authorHOUSE®

AuthorHouse™
1663 Liberty Drive
Bloomington, IN 47403
www.authorhouse.com
Phone: 1-800-839-8640

© 2011 Daniel W. Bena
First published by AuthorHouse 11/01/2011
ISBN 978-1-4520-6541-0 (sc)
ISBN: 978-1-4670-3346-6 (e)
Library of Congress Control Number: 2010911939

Printed in the United States of America.

This book is printed on acid-free paper.

Because of the dynamic nature of the Internet, any Web addresses or links
contained in this book may have changed since publication and may no longer
be valid. The views expressed in this work are solely those of the author
and do not necessarily reflect the views of the publisher or PepsiCo, and
the publisher and PepsiCo hereby disclaims any responsibility for them.

Table of Contents

For my Tar

About This Book

A few words about this book—specifically, about the sustainable practices that were used to produce it. One of the major reasons I chose iuniverse.com to self-publish this book is because they were able to accommodate my request for action—action toward a book that not only conveys useful information in the content, but that is also an example of that content in its own publishing process. They really "stepped up to the plate," and found a great publisher in the US.

A book of this nature, with this subject matter, almost by definition brings with it high expectations. It was critical to me, as an impassioned author, that the physical document reflect the internal content. It needed to be genuine and credible, and to be both of those, it needed to "practice what it preaches."

I worked with the great teams at iuniverse.com to identify what we believe is the printer with the most comprehensive sustainable practices in their system. As a result, this book was produced using what are among the most robust operational practices available here in the US. For example:

- 100% of the black text ink is soy or vegetable oil-based ink
- The interior is printed on 50% recycled stock
- The cover is printed on Sustainable Forestry Initiative-certified forest friendly paper
- Efficient compact fluorescent light bulbs (CFLs) are used in the manufacturing facility. In addition, in the facility used, manufacturing waste that had traditionally been thrown away is currently being reclaimed for other uses. The following items are completely reclaimed for future use:
  - 100% of post-production paper, segmented as printed/unprinted, and free of unground sheets
  - All waste/unusable ink
  - All aluminum printing plates
  - All silver from film development, film scraps, and the recycling of old titles

- All waste sludge, reclaimed using an in-house solvent recycler
- All used oil
- All steel
- All plastic wrap, straps, drums, and bottles
- All old computer hardware
- All used toner cartridges
- All defective books
- All book cloth

The printer is constantly looking for new ways to rethink, reduce, and reuse manufacturing byproducts. From paper dust used as bedding for horses, to the complete recycling of all returns, they strive to maximize recycling value. This result is one of the smallest eco-footprints available in this industry, and a book of which I am proud since it "practices what it preaches."

Preface

Hopefully, the title of this book captured your attention enough to have you open it and read this preface. What, you might ask, gives me license to write about sustainable development for the corporate world? I suppose the best answer is one-word: passion.

Allow me to share a brief conversation I had recently with PepsiCo's Chair and CEO, Indra Nooyi. First off, please realize that she is truly an enlightened one when it comes to understanding and implementing sustainability programs within the context of a business—and a large, multinational business at that (PepsiCo currently enjoys a turnover of approximately sixty billion dollars annually, and employs a veritable army of nearly 300,000 associates worldwide). But back to the story. Indra was kind enough to seat me next to her at a Board of Directors' dinner—surely a seat of honor—and over the course of the evening, we talked about sustainability. I was moved to share with her that I have found my niche. Actually, so much more than a niche. I explained to her that for the first 20 years of my PepsiCo career, I had what I would describe as a great job, which certainly paid the mortgage and allowed my wife and me to live comfortably. In the past five years, though, coinciding to when sustainability became formalized at PepsiCo, I told Indra that I discovered my passion.

Now, please realize that for a long time, I was a typical scientist—not very emotionally-driven, hyper-analytical (sometimes to a fault)-- and I was never really one of those people who heralded the importance of "finding your passion in a job," or "doing something that you love." To me, "love," after all was something reserved for my wife, and family, and pets…not my job. Well, this is most likely because I didn't know what being passionate about a job really entailed. It's sort of a not-so-secret club, which is hard to describe. It's not as if you could give someone a recipe to find his or her passion; indeed, you can't teach the process in the classroom. But, rest assured, once you find it, you know it, and it becomes transformative. And "transform" is precisely what happened to me once I found a part of my job about which I am passionate.

When I started at PepsiCo in 1984, it was literally to take a job—any job—that would allow me to make enough money to help put my wife through medical school. The plan was for her to finish med school, and then for me to attend medical school, supported by her salary as a physician. To make a very long story short, I never applied to medical school. And I never really left PepsiCo in 25 years. I say "really" because there was this interesting six month period in 1989 when I thought my "elite" biochemistry degree was being wasted working for a soda company, so I became an environmental organic chemist. Hated it! I couldn't wait to return to PepsiCo, and return I did.

Even more interesting along the lines of "transformation," though, is the actual metamorphosis of my core personality which occurred—driven by what I found to be my passion. You see, when I began with PepsiCo, I was the premier model of a scientific introvert—insecure in everything but my scientific knowledge, intimidated at the thought of having to use my interpersonal skills, never wanting to leave the laboratory. I wore a brown, three-piece suit—a sign of executive "weakness"—during a time in corporate America when all of the real leaders were wearing navy blue suits, white shirts, and burgundy ties (who says there was no uniform for corporate America in the 1980s?). My idea of adventure was leaving the lab—almost never alone, but always with one or both of my great friends, Rob or Lynda—simply to go to the office part of the building to enjoy a cup of coffee! How ridiculous, in retrospect, but you know what they say about hindsight being 20/20!

How did discovering my passion transform my core personality? I said that I was an insecure introvert then. Now, people have a really difficult time shutting me up. Over the years, I have had the great fortune—and I say this from the heart—of being able to address many audiences around the world on the topic of sustainable development. This is all thanks to PepsiCo...all of it, and I am forever thankful. My beloved mentor at PepsiCo, Harry DeLonge, in addition to teaching me all the science behind water treatment and chemistry, also taught me life lessons, which I think are so much more important. One piece of sage counsel was about the importance of humility and grounding. Long before my first external speaking engagement, Harry said, "You are going to find that a lot of doors will open for you, Dan, and you must always remember that while Dan Bena has a little to do with it, the doors open because of PepsiCo." I have never forgotten that, and firmly believe it.

My zeal is passion-fueled. Once you find your passion, you realize that there are literally not enough hours in the day to help fulfill it. And it is remarkably helpful to have a loving spouse who understands and tolerates this, as I do in my wife, Diane!

1

Context: Looking Through the Lens of the Triple Bottom Line

If you've already purchased this book, chances are good that you have at least some familiarity with the concept of the Triple Bottom Line. If not, no worries. I approach this concept very simply, recognizing that the impact can be far reaching.

We've all heard the phrase "the bottom line," indicating the foundational profitability of a business. It can also indicate a way to get directly to the point of a conversation, as in "what's the bottom line?" Both interpretations are applicable to the concept of the "Triple Bottom Line."

The phrase itself is generally credited as having been coined by John Elkington in his 1998 book entitled,

Cannibals with Forks: The Triple Bottom Line of 21st Century Business. Many definitions and interpretations have followed since, but one of the more alliterative is the idea of the "three Ps: People, Planet, and Profit." Each is fairly intuitive, and are also discussed in the more specific terms, *Society (People), Environment (Planet), and Economy (Profit).*

In short, the triple bottom line is an attempt at a quantitative business model which would expand the traditional measure of business profitability (revenue) to include elements which include respect for people and the environment. This might sound simple, but it is no small task. The biggest challenge lies in the word "quantitative." Included in this term are metrics—ways to monitor a company's performance beyond self-reported anecdote. Ideally, the metrics should be robust, representative of what it is they are trying to convey, and—most importantly in the context of the triple bottom line—comparable from one company to another. The intent, just like with a financial bottom line, is to be able to compare the overall "health" of a company against its peers and competitors, but this time including metrics for social and environmental performance, in addition to financial performance.

Recognizing the challenges of foreign currency exchange and how this often complicates financial reporting for industry, especially for a large multinational, the metrics to report financial performance are—by and large—uniform worldwide. The same is not true for the metrics associated with the other two elements of the triple bottom line--society and environment. In this book, I will not delve deeply into the specific challenges associated with these metrics, but it is important for the reader to know that they are in their infancy. Many companies, academics, consultants, non-governmental organizations (NGOs), and even governments, are trying diligently to develop and harmonize these metrics, but we are only at the beginning of this journey.

This next section offers an illustrative explanation of an important concept. Figure 1 shows the way the elements of the triple bottom line are often depicted. Society, economy, and environment are represented as three circles drawn with equal diameter, overlapping toward the center. This center, often referred to as "the sweet spot,"

Figure 1. Traditional Depiction of the Triple Bottom Line

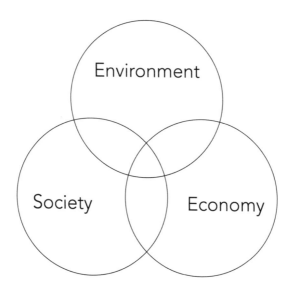

is the point at which the interests of society, economy, and environment intersect—presumably implying that it is in this space where a win/win/win for all three elements may be found. This idea is, indeed, illustrative, but the concept of the sweet spot is absolutely core to the pursuit of a robust triple bottom line. Noted author and good friend, Andy Savitz, in his book entitled, The Triple Bottom Line, does a masterful job describing the positive benefits of engaging in this sweet spot, and provides an informative primer of the intersecting circles model of the triple bottom line.

Note the graphic change in Figure 2. The text within the circles is the same as that in Figure 1, but the circles are not intersecting—nor are they equally sized. I first saw this depiction from one of my colleagues at PepsiCo in the United Kingdom, a true sustainability "illuminatum,"—a guy who "gets it." In fact, a few years ago, this model was shared publicly in the first Environmental Sustainability Report ever issued by our UK business, and it has resonated remarkably well with many audiences since then.

The circles are neither equally sized nor intersecting—for a reason. Starting at the center and moving outward, we see society—the collection of people in communities that are so important for quality of life. Society includes the richness and diversity of culture, education, art, language, and so much more. Clearly, people are critically important to the model, and thus are depicted at the core. Societies, as they interact and develop, form economies...

Figure 2. Alternate Depiction of Triple Bottom Line

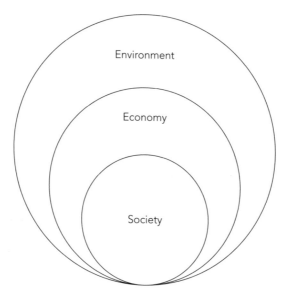

at both micro and macro levels. Important, certainly, but without people, without society, there would be no economy. The final and outer-most ring depicts the environment. This is not to indicate a greater relative importance of planet over people, but merely to emphasize the interdependence. If the planet falls prey to a cataclysmic event, economy and society become moot. Simply put, if the planet fails, so do people, and everything associated with them.

This sounds a bit ominous, and perhaps melodramatic, but I challenge you to disagree with the premise. Some—many, in fact—would argue that the current and impending climate crises with which the world is faced are precisely those cataclysmic events described above!

So, fine. A company needs to address all three elements

of the triple bottom line. But how? This is so much more easily said (or written) than done. The "triple bottom line" is more than a model; more than a few circles on a page, whether they are depicted as concentric or interlinked. The "triple bottom line" is a framework—a visionary, yet very much "common sense" framework for how companies can increase their chances of success for years—decades—maybe even centuries to come. In its simplest form, the "Triple Bottom Line" illustrates that companies are not islands. They are not isolated, and do not exist alone. They do not sit "apart from" society and economy; rather, they are "a part of" them. In fact, they can be significant parts of both society and the economic health of that society.

The rest of this book will address many aspects of this concept in more detail—with realistic actions you can take to get moving on a sustainable development journey. For now, we'll start slowly, with some questions to consider. Think about how you would answer these questions now, before reading the rest of this book, and then ask yourself these same questions again once you've finished the book. Hopefully, the answers will be different, which would mean that the content of the book caused you to consider things a bit differently than you do now.

Questions to consider, for a start:

1. What does "sustainability" mean to you?
2. Are "sustainability" and "sustainable development" synonymous? Why or why not? (You

knew it couldn't be as simple as a "yes" or "no"!)

3. Do only large companies benefit from having a strategy for sustainable development?

4. Is "sustainability" all about protecting the environment?

5. "Sustainability" is a buzz word, and many folks are interested in it, but do I really believe in it, or is it a "flavor of the month" that will pass like so many other things?

Once again, spend some time — a few minutes. You can afford a few minutes! Ask yourself these questions, and answer them — honestly. Don't answer them the way you THINK you should answer them, i.e., to be "politically correct," and don't answer them the way you think your CEO would like you to answer them! No one has to know what your answers are except you, so do a little soul searching. Bringing your answers to top of mind will help increase your own awareness as you go through the rest of this book.

Okay, that's the only attempt at amateur psychoanalysis you will find in this book—I promise...maybe.

Key Take-Aways from Chapter One

1. The Triple Bottom Line is a model based on the traditional concept of the financial bottom line and was devised to help quantitatively compare companies among their peers and competitors.

2. The Triple Bottom Line expands what is expected in the definition of a "profitable business" to include not only the financial performance and how it contributes to economy, but also the softer side of performance: how a company contributes to society and helps protect the environment.

3. Different models exist that paint the elements of the triple bottom line—society, economy, and environment--with an equal brush, but recognize that if the planet fails, society and economy cease to exist.

4. The triple bottom line is more than a model on a piece of paper. It is—or can be—a very valuable concept for how businesses should conduct their day-to-day activities to assure success for decades to come.

2

Sustainability vs. Sustainable Development: Are They the Same?

One (at least!) of the questions in the previous chapter was a "trick" question to hopefully lead you down a thought path.

Now that we are all on the same proverbial page in terms of the concept of the triple bottom line, it's time to address what might seem to some as semantics, but to practitioners in this space is an important nuance to distinguish. Often, the terms "sustainability" and "sustainable development" are used synonymously and interchangeably, but, as the chapter title asks, are they the same?

Five years ago or so, if you asked me that question, I

would have said, "Absolutely. They are the same." You choose which term to use based on how much space you have to fill on a Powerpoint slide, right? If you have a lot of room, "sustainable development" works well to fill it. Today, I use this question as a filter; a person's answer indicates to me his/her understanding of the topic—whether they are in this as part of a business imperative (which is certainly good if it results in positive impact), or whether they are, like the colleague I described in Chapter One, one of the true "illuminati" in this area.

What do I mean by such a bold, almost arrogant, statement? From the outset, please understand that, regardless of whether you use the term "sustainability," or "sustainable development," what really matters is that the company involved is taking steps to improve their triple bottom line. That is, in addition to assuring sound financial performance of their company, they also have initiatives in place to materially help protect the environment and also improve the lives of the people who form our local and global societies. That said, many people—particularly in the corporate world—tend to use "sustainability" as the terminology of choice. Apart from the fact that the term itself rolls off the tongue a bit more smoothly than the more awkward "sustainable development," they are typically referring to programs which will help assure the "sustainability" of their business by funding programs that include helping society and the planet. In this case, the benefits to society and environment are important, but secondary.

In contrast to their private sector corporate counterparts, practitioners from non-government organizations and non-profit entities generally opt for the term "sustainable development." This refers less to the "sustainability" of the business, as in the first description, and more to the sustainability of society as being paramount. Only by assuring that society is thriving, communities are healthy, and the planet is respected, will you have a truly sustainable business. Different from the first description above, "sustainable development" places development of society and protection of planet as front and center—in fact, identifies them as the drivers which will assure a sustainable business. It's sort of the chicken and the egg scenario—which comes first.

In the end, does it matter? It may. In this book, I will generally "flex," and use both terms, depending on the message of each chapter. However, as you yourself engage in discussing this fascinating topic, it is important that you understand the lexicon, and are able to "flex" with your audience. This understated nuance between terms could mean the difference between making an audience bristle with a lack of receptivity, or recognizing the speaker as credible, and immediately becoming more open to dialog and engagement. Now, I'm not naïve enough to pin success or failure on a single nuance, but this one is important. It's akin to another current phrase—the acronym "BOP," which is used to refer to the billions of people living in abject poverty who are often viewed as potential markets for businesses. The acronym which refers to them is "BOP." Some interpret the "B" as meaning "bottom"—that is, the "bottom of the pyramid." A negative connotation to those poor, unfortunate people...not far from the metaphor of "dregs" that settle to the bottom. A much more positive, and I believe accurate, definition of the "B" is as "base" of the pyramid. This indicates that this population is responsible for the strong, unbreakable integrity of the very foundation of the pyramid. The pyramids, after all, are one of the most enduring structures of our time. I hope you will agree that it's more than just semantics.

I would be remiss if I didn't mention one last thought about "sustainable development." The word "development" is also shared by the "Millennium Development Goals," or MDGs. If you are, or want to be, serious about understanding sustainable development, you must recognize the MDGs. These are a set of eight goals, developed by the United Nations and publicized at the beginning of the new millennium in 2000, which were intended to help lift the world out of poverty. From their own website:

"In September 2000, building upon a decade of major United Nations conferences and summits, world leaders came together at United Nations Headquarters in New York to adopt the United Nations Millennium Declaration, committing their nations to a new global partnership to reduce extreme poverty and setting out a series of time-bound targets - with a deadline of 2015 - that have become known as the Millennium Development Goals."

The beauty and power of the MDGs is that they are holistic and far-reaching. They tackle the causes of extreme poverty at their very foundation, e.g., maternal health, infant illnesses, and access to safe water. I won't spend a lot of time discussing the MDGs beyond introducing them above, but I do encourage you to "Google" them and learn more about them. There are links on www.danbena.com, as well.

Key Take-Aways from Chapter Two

1. The difference between the terms "sustainability" and "sustainable development" is more than just semantics.

2. "Sustainability" is used more often by people from private industry, and implies the sustainability of their business which will result from funding and leading societal and environmental initiatives.

3. "Sustainable Development" is used more often by people from non-profit entities and other non-government organizations, and places the development of society and protection of environment as paramount. Positive benefits to business will be secondary, and a direct result of societal and environmental efforts.

3

Where Does Sustainability Fit With Corporate Responsibility Programs?

One of the things with which many companies grapple is understanding the distinction between Sustainability and Corporate Responsibility agendas. Some wonder whether a distinction is really needed, or is one merely a subset of the other? The "short answer" —as you might expect—is that all companies do not address this topic in the same manner. Some look at "sustainability" as being synonymous with "environmental sustainability," and, as such, have a very acute focus on the conservation of the natural resources they use. Certainly, proper utilization of resources is an important element of stewardship, which also relates to the expectations of a corporation to act responsibly.

Other companies, however, expand their approach to "sustainability" to extend far beyond environment—more like what we discussed in the previous chapter—on the road to programs in "sustainable development." Here, the concept of the triple bottom line discussed earlier plays a much more prominent role. In these cases, companies' "Corporate Responsibility" (also called "corporate social responsibility; CSR") programs generally include some form of societal / community development, in addition to being stewards of the environment. This could be supporting education in communities, improving literacy, promoting health and wellness; many possibilities exist to the creative practitioners of corporate responsibility.

A colleague of mine at PepsiCo, Claire Lyons, has provided me with sage counsel on this topic over the years. Claire manages the environmental portfolio of the company's PepsiCo Foundation, traditionally seen as the philanthropic arm of the corporation. Over the course of many dialogs, Claire has crystallized a model which she has coined the "Purpose Spectrum," named for the PepsiCo operating model called Performance with Purpose, about which you will read more in subsequent chapters.

As the following figure illustrates, at one end of the spectrum is what is called "100% charitable purpose"— in other words, what most would think of as traditional

Figure 3. The Purpose Spectrum

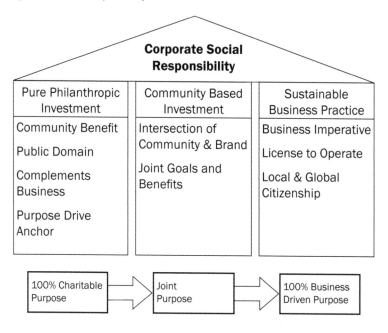

philanthropy, which has long been an important tool for companies to help activate and implement their corporate responsibility programs. This purely philanthropic investment model is the closest to what we call "writing the proverbial check" to an organization—usually a non-profit or academic entity—to help support a laudable cause. Usually, but not always, this model is fairly linear—that is, the grantor provides direct funding to the grantee or beneficiary of the funds, and the grantor then generally relegates control of the money to the grantee or beneficiary. In other words, there is not much collaborative dialog in this model once the funding is provided. This is still a positive approach, particularly for the poorest of the poor, or in response to catastrophes, like natural disasters, where financial aid is urgently needed. The genuine applications for this model, though, are becoming fewer and fewer.

At the other end of the spectrum in this illustration is what we are calling "100% Business Driven Purpose." In other words, projects that are the result of direct business funding. As its title implies, in this model, the funding for corporate social responsibility initiatives comes exclusively from direct lines of business. For example, for a consumer product, a brand marketing budget might support funding a community initiative with direct linkage to the brand. In another example, perhaps a company's Communications Department might fund a literacy improvement project for underprivileged children. In these cases, there is no involvement of a Foundation, or a more philanthropic entity of the company. A great example of this end of the spectrum is a campaign which PepsiCo launched in 2010, called the "Pepsi Refresh Campaign" (*www.refresheverything.com*). In this model, which has received positive acclaim from many interested groups, part of a brand marketing budget (the brand being traditional Pepsi-Cola carbonated beverage) is used to fund projects that will help improve the world. In this program, consumers are invited to submit proposals for grants—ranging from $5,000 to $250,000 every month—for projects about which they are passionate, and which are intended to improve the world in some way. They can be health related, environmental, social—virtually anything that can make a difference in the world. Then, the submitters are charged with letting everyone know about their submission, and solicit people to vote on a website for their projects. The projects with the most votes win the grants. In 2010, the company estimates that it will give away over $20 million in these refresh grants. Again—from a Marketing budget. Not a single cent contributed from traditional philanthropy. I strongly believe (and increasingly more and more folks agree) that this model is the way of the future.

In the middle of the Purpose Spectrum, and this is really a continuum, there is the combination—the hybrid of more traditional philanthropic funding and the more progressive linkage to the business. This is a critical concept to understand and respect, for a couple of reasons. First, from a regulatory perspective in the United States and other countries, the funding from a corporate Foundation is often strictly controlled by tax laws. Depending on the rigor with which your corporate tax counsel interprets these applicable laws, the approach could range from conservative, where the efforts of the Foundation are kept so isolated from the business that documents don't even mention both on the same page— to more liberal, where the efforts of a Foundation still comply unquestionably with the law, but are arranged to complement and support analogous areas of focus by the business. Admittedly, the latter case presents a sometimes contentious balance which must be struck, and necessitates all projects being evaluated on a case-by-case basis.

The second reason why this distinction is critical relates to the way Foundation-funded initiatives are perceived by external stakeholders. Read that last line again—it is important, and was to me a surprising lesson that I learned by experience. It may seem like a paradox in some ways, but certain groups—typically the more aggressive / activist NGOs and, more recently, the investment community—have come to almost dismiss the efforts of a company if they are funded philanthropically from a Foundation. This is ironic, and unfortunate, because the projects funded by Foundations often target very different populations than those targeted by business initiatives. In addition, the communication efforts are often also targeted to different audiences or through different channels.

At issue is the fact that, due to the strict tax control to which Foundations are subject, groups often equate Foundation funding with a tax loophole. While companies might enjoy tax benefits from foundation funding streams, the projects are none the less laudable, and the beneficiaries none the less deserving. In fact, one could argue that if a company were to be given relief from tax liability for philanthropic projects, this would potentially make more funding available for such projects than if the tax relief did not exist.

The decision, of course, must be made by the individual

company, but those that have proven the most success-ful are those that have struck the right balance between traditional philanthropy and direct business funding of community initiatives. You'll find this "striking the right balance" to be a consistent theme throughout this book. Some of this is due to my personal belief that balance is a good thing; the rest is due to the natural order. Rarely, in nature, do things exist as absolutes—or at the poles of a spectrum. Like water, things in nature usually seek their own level, and this level is usually toward equilibrium. This hybrid—or balanced--approach is often referred to as "smart" or "strategic" philanthropy.

Can philanthropy really be "strategic"? You'd better believe it! Just as a company develops business plans to activate their business strategies, so they should with philanthropic efforts. Just as a successful business strate-gy generally focuses on the core capabilities of a business, so should a successful philanthropic strategy. Consider this hypothetical example: A company's core business depends on their use of land—say, to grow some new crop to be used to make artificial leather (I'm creating as I go along, so bear with me!). One of the company's international business segments, as part of its decentral-ized philanthropic strategy, decided to donate bed nets to children in communities that suffer from mosquito-transmitted malaria. A great cause, right? Who could argue that? Helping to prevent deaths from malarial dis-eases with something as simple as a bed net? BUT, is this an example of smart or strategic philanthropy? Arguably, no. The business has nothing to do with healthcare, or children, or flying insect control—so where is the smart link to the business? There is none. "Smart" philanthropic strategies and plans are those that *complement* and *support* the core capability or strategic direction of the business. In this example, instead of donating bed nets, it would be very strategic to develop partnerships to help assure that the new crop the company was growing was being grown in a way that protected the rights of the people on the farms, or that preserved the use of natural resources used to grow the crop. If, instead of this new crop being used to make artificial leather, it was going to be used to develop a new anti-malarial drug, which would take several years to commercialize, then maybe the bed nets would be a strategic approach. Helping short-term to stem the spread of malarial disease with bed nets, with the longer-term view of developing robust antimalarials. Again—this would provide the critical linkage of the company's philanthropic community efforts to the same company's business needs. "Strategic philanthropy."

A closely related concept, and one which has formally evolved only recently, is that of "social investment." This represents a great combination of a "social" element (as in the triple bottom line, and related to sustainable development) and an "investment" element, which would certainly resonate strongly with the more business minded leaders among us. If, in fact, we are investing in society, it follows that all responsible businesses would expect a tangible "return" on that investment. Clearly the return on investment (ROI) for social or environmental projects is not as easily calculated as those projects subjected to traditional financial ROI, but can be just as important.

Being able to calculate an ROI on a social investment portfolio of partners or projects allows corporate responsibility or sustainability practitioners to speak the same language as leaders of industry. By using this same lexicon, social investments are brought into the same playing field and elevated to the same level of importance as the more traditional financial investments; this is critical to the success of CSR programs. Let me say this again, because this is one of the most important concepts in this book: it is absolutely critical that social investments by a corporation be treated with the same level of rigor, importance, and respect by senior leadership as are financial investments. The minute that a social investment program is relegated to secondary or "nice to have" status marks the death knell for the program. In the long run, the business will suffer the consequences.

This discussion is way more than just an intellectual exercise. As we look to the future—to maintain and retain a competitive advantage—the private sector will need to continue to think and act creatively. In the US, an interesting movement is emerging—one called the "B corporation." There are several classifications of private businesses in the US, but this is a new one. The "B" stands for "Benefit" and implies that the purpose of a "B corporation" is about more than making money. It suggests that B Corporations have responsibility not only to their shareholders, but to a larger audience of stakeholders as well. From the B-corporation website (*www.bcorporation.net*):

> "Certified B Corporations are a new type of corporation which uses the power of business to solve social and environmental problems. B Corps are unlike traditional businesses because they:
>
> Meet comprehensive and transparent social and environmental performance standards;
>
> Meet higher legal accountability standards;
>
> Build business constituency for good business "

According to the same website, there are already 327 certified B-corporations in the United States, representing 54 industries and $1.6 billion in combined revenue. This idea is taking on such genuine interest, in fact, that in 2010, the States of Maryland and Vermont passed legislation recognizing the nomenclature of the "B-corporation." Perhaps a hint of things to come.

So, getting back to the title of this chapter, a successful company in this space is one that has the foresight and bold vision to leverage the concept of Corporate Social Responsibility as the overarching program, under which all related sustainability programs fall. Accomplishing this and making CSR a core element of the business helps embed it in the day-to-day processes and systems used to run the business. As my colleague, Claire, often heralds, "CSR cannot be seen as something *additional* to the business; it must be seen as something that *is* the business." Heed these sound words of advice.

So, by now, you hopefully understand the Triple Bottom Line, and how critical it is for companies to espouse, and acknowledge the nuance between the concepts of "sustainability" and "sustainable development." You also should have a pretty good feel for the differences between sustainability and corporate responsibility, as well as smart philanthropy vs. social investment. Great. But, if you are reading this as an associate of a company—large or small, uni- or multi-national—and you are interested in beginning a sustainability journey or accelerating the one you are already on, how do you structure for sustainable development?

A tough question...kind of. It really depends on what the purpose is for the structure (objectives, end-goals, etc.), and also where your company is along its sustainability journey. It also depends on the resources that are available, both human and financial, and the areas on which you would like to focus—strategically. Some might think the simplest answer is to appoint a Chief Sustainability Officer, and let him or her solve the problems. Certainly, many companies have gone this route, especially at the

Figure 4. The Four Steps to Sustainability

Four Steps to Sustainability			
Customer demand frequently triggers corporate sustainability programs. The table below describes the four steps that typically occur as customer demand transforms into a formal program.			
1	**2**	**3**	**4**
Customer Demand	Business Unit Response	Executive "Aha!"	Sustainability Program
Customer demand for sustainability products, services, and/ or processes typically enters company through individual business units.	Individual Business Units respond to customer demand independently and soon roll up sustainability initiatives into their individual strategies.	The CEO or another member of the executive team recognizes the push for sustainability in different parts of the business.	In response, the CEO/Executive Team creates an umbrella organization and appoints a Chief Sustainability Officer to more effectively manage and leverage disparate sustainability messages and efforts across the enterprise.

beginnings of their journeys. However, in my experience, the more successful approach is for a Chief Sustainability Officer position to evolve into being. In general, added layers of management for a company are not good for efficiency or effectiveness, and you must remember this for a sustainability architecture as well. Not to say that companies shouldn't have a central function to manage sustainability, but this function should be well-thought, carefully-considered, and most likely—lean. A couple of years ago, the well-known executive recruiting agency, Korn-Ferry, through the Korn-Ferry Institute, published a brief, easily-digestible white paper, entitled, "Why, and

How, Companies Create Sustainability Programs and Appoint Chief Sustainability Officers." In this paper, they do a great job summarizing the four stages of evolution, which really resonated with me, and which I believe apply quite broadly. Figure 4 illustrates this evolution.

While I believe this is broadly applicable to many companies, I don't mean to suggest that this is the best way to evolve. It just seems to be a common one, perhaps because the formalized discipline of sustainable development as it relates to business is relatively new. In many ways, businesses are formulating "rules" as they go along. There weren't many existing standards or business practices in this area even ten years ago—but many have been developed, and are continuing to be.

Key Take-Aways from Chapter Three

1. There are many points along the Purpose Spectrum at which companies can activate their corporate responsibility programs. Striking the proper balance between traditional philanthropy and business funding is key.

2. In the US and other countries, funding by a corporate Foundation is strictly regulated by tax law. You must understand these laws completely, and interpret them in a way that allows Foundation strategies to *complement* the strategies of the business.

3. Finding ways to calculate an ROI for social investments, just as businesses would calculate an ROI for financial investments, is critical to accelerate the acceptance and success of corporate responsibility programs.

4. Front running companies are those that have already heeded the advice of my colleague: "CSR cannot be seen as something *additional* to the business; it must be seen as something that *is* the business."

5. To "do" sustainability properly, as with anything, companies need a structure to manage it and the resources to support it. The structure could range from a lean central function headed by a Chief Sustainability Officer, to cross-business, interconnected Committees or Councils to provide the needed thought leadership to the business. Many architectures can be effective, but it depends on the goals, focus areas, and objectives of the function.

4

What Are Consumers Around the World Expecting Of Companies?

Let's start this chapter with a couple of questions to establish a very important basic premise: how do you get elected officials to act? How do you get consumer products companies to act?

Hopefully, the answers to both are intuitive, and you were able to answer both with a few moments' thought. Here's my point of view. For officials to act effectively, they must know what is important to the majority of their constituents—the potential voters who might be moved to elect or re-elect them. This is precisely why grassroots petitions can be so influential, and an example of where the internet has really unleashed a groundswell of organized public opinion. Just moments ago, I "Googled" the phrase "on-line petitions," and discovered no fewer than 4.9 million hits! People have clearly realized the importance of conveying an organized message. Whether it has to do with saving the rainforests, conserving water, or battling chronic malnutrition, the old adage "there is power in numbers" is more true now than ever. The internet has allowed these "numbers" to amass virtually, to great effect.

Now, for the second question: how do you get consumer products companies to act? This becomes much easier, given the rationale of the first reply, but to put it simply, you get consumer products companies to act by getting enough consumers to want a particular product. This is very analogous to the elected official scenario, but the constituents in this case are the consumers. It's obvious, but bears stating—if consumers go away, so does the company that supplies them. To ignore the customer is to face corporate extinction. As you will see, this is true not only of the specific product choices that consumers make; consumers have become much more sophisticated and zealous, and their expectations have entered the realm of sustainable development.

To illustrate how broad these expectations are, let's start with Figure 5, which comes from a global survey company called Globescan. They are a leading voice in surveys dealing with corporate responsibility and sustainability, and the rigor with which they control their

Figure 5. Consumers' Expectations of Companies

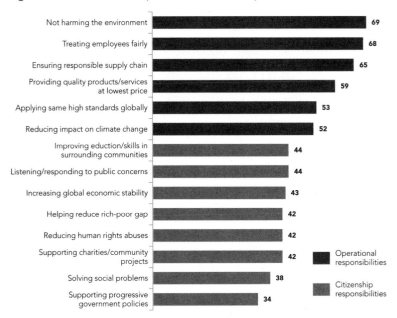

Courtesy Globescan, 2010. All rights served

data collection results in an error of approximately +/- 3%. In this case, Globescan asked people across 25 countries the following question: "For what do you hold companies completely responsible?" Keep in mind, I specifically said the survey group was "people"—not specifically political constituents or any one consumer segment—so the answers are broadly applicable. The replies, detailed in Figure 5, were eye-opening for me and for many of my colleagues.

What was particularly eye-opening, which is not explicit from this chart but which comes through in the detailed report from Globescan, is the similarity of responses across most of the countries surveyed. This includes respondents in developed and developing countries alike. The bottom line is that people everywhere, for the most part, are holding companies "completely responsible" for (1) protecting and not harming the environment, (2) treating people well, and (3) providing safe, high quality products.

This is elegant simplicity at its best, since these expectations fit perfectly within the boundaries of sustainable development that I introduced previously, called the Triple Bottom Line (economy, society, and environment). The Globescan study, in my opinion, is a landmark one, and points the way very clearly for companies across the globe. There are many, many more studies that provide insight into what the general public and specific consumers expect from companies. Because this text is intended to be crisp and to give sustainability novices and practitioners the basic foundation of what they need to accelerate a sustainability program, these will not be discussed here. However, references to them may be found on my website, www.danbena.com. One other thing worth mentioning, which is largely a phenomenon—at least currently—of developed economies (for example, US, Canada, United Kingdom and others), is a consumer segment known as "LOHAS." LOHAS stands for "Lifestyles of Health and Sustainability" and is an increasing segment in many geographies. According to the website, www. lohas.com, the LOHAS segment is "a market segment focused on health and fitness, the environment, personal development, sustainable living, and social justice," which really says it all. These consumers are extremely educated on the topics of sustainable development, and can discuss many of the issues in great depth. Many are also at the upper end of the economic scale, which means that they can pay a premium for the products that meet their demands. In addition, many are "millennials—members of the so-called "generation Y"—the demographic segment that includes people born between 1980 and 2000 (give or take a few years). Millennials are often less interested in financial gain, being driven by a greater cause. This passion also brings with it very clear expectations of companies, governments, peers, and just about everything else. Make no mistake, Millennials know what is important to them, are laser-focused on how to get it, and can be quite impatient if the world doesn't move quickly enough to suit their expectations. If you don't know about Millennials, you would do well to find out—fast!

If you work for a company, especially a publicly-held company, you learn very quickly that there are MANY different stakeholders. Consumers of your products, or clients of your services, are obviously very important, and can have a very influential voice. In addition, however, we must recognize the influence that the "influencers" can have. Influencers are usually those individuals or groups that are the thought leaders for a particular topic, and are given the name because their opinions—which are usually, but not always, very vocal—influence the thoughts and actions of others. The same company that provided the figure mentioned earlier, Globescan, not only surveys the general populace across the world. They also routinely identify, vet, and survey recognized experts in the field of sustainable development. These data are critical complements to the other data, since the opinions of the experts often provide a foreshadowing of what the opinions of the general population will be a year or two down the road. In one of their most recent surveys (made jointly with another great organization, SustainAbility), conducted during March and April of 2010, they included over 1200 recognized sustainability experts representing 80 countries across the world. So, very current, and very robust.

Several strong messages emerged from this expert survey: (1) There is a strong sense of urgency to address numerous and diverse sustainable development challenges; (2) The most urgent issues are highly inter-connected, which implies the need to take a systems approach to addressing sustainability, rather than developing narrow solutions for specific issues; and (3) Across nearly all industries, water and energy-related issues are cited as the most important for business to address. Figure 6 illustrates the areas of urgency in the minds of this cross-section of sustainability experts. Numbers in the graph represent percentages of respondents who believe the issue on the left axis are either "very" or "somewhat" urgent.

So, you get it—and you may have already known it

subconsciously: your company brings with it MANY stakeholders. Some are more influential than others, some more vocal, and some more rational. As a company, you need to identify and map these stakeholders, then decide which to engage. It's okay to make a decision NOT to engage some of them. Many companies make the mistake of thinking that absolutely every stakeholder—and, indeed, every critic—needs to be engaged and made part of the dialog. Not true. This was a tough lesson for me to learn personally, and it took several years—and several mistakes—for me to learn it. There are several diagrams available in the literature regarding stakeholder

Figure 6. Urgency of Environmental and Social Crises

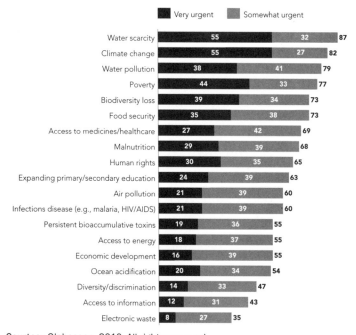

engagement that try to assess a variety of factors, e.g., openness, receptivity, value, influence, and others. In my opinion, and what I often tell folks, is that if a stakeholder is willing to open the door to genuine dialog even a little bit—just crack the door enough to let some light shine through—then I am willing to engage. The hard lesson I learned—and even now I still hate to admit it—is that there are people and groups who will NEVER open that door. They will expect you to speak to them—more accurately, THEY will expect to speak to YOU—through a closed door, with no dialog, no "give and take," and then expect you to do precisely what they ask. This is not healthy, it is not efficient, it is not effective, and it is not value-added for the company or its associates who are trying to engage. In these instances, the best advice is to recognize the stakeholder as non-engaging, or non-collaborative, and move on to those stakeholders who are!

Back to the "power in numbers" approach. Whether you are a small company or a large multinational, numbers are powerful on many levels. As stated above, collaboration among individuals and groups can combine to form a formidable voice, but there is also a more quantitative power in numbers. Not only do consumers, political constituents, and many other stakeholder groups expect companies to do the things already described in this chapter—to remind you: protect the planet, treat people well, and assure safe and high quality products—they also expect companies to be able to establish goals, and communicate progress toward these goals. The old saying goes, "you can't manage what you don't measure." This is absolutely sage advice. Recognizing that the journey could be a long one for some companies, every one needs to start—and the start needs to include credible metrics; the data upon which your performance is judged. This might sound easier than it ends up being in reality.

The data and metrics around the elements of sustainable development are often lumped into one of two broad categories—"non-financial metrics." The other category, of course, is "financial metrics." On the financial side, while it can become complex when dealing in foreign currencies and exchange rates, by and large the rules exist to report financial performance—and these rules are fairly uniform globally. In its simplest form, think of a balance sheet: debits and credits. There may be different interpretations as to what qualifies for a debit and credit, but in the end, the rules of the game are understood, and the auditing and verification systems are in place to help assure accurate, credible reporting.

On the "non-financial" metrics side, these assurance systems and uniform processes are only now beginning to be formulated. The complexity is enormous and the task daunting…and there are many, many consulting agencies working hard to develop "the best" approach. As an example, take something as simple as water use measurements. You would think that it is easy to measure the water that comes into a facility and the water that leaves the facility, right? In theory, maybe. But consider these variables:

- Is it municipal water? Is the meter correct? If so, has it ever been calibrated? What is the variability in the measurement?
- If it is not a municipal supply, is there a meter on the well? Does it work? How do you know?
- How do you account for evaporation losses during the process? What percentage do you choose? How do you measure it?
- How do you measure wastewater being discharged? My engineer colleagues tell me that you can get significantly different numbers if you use a meter, vs. a weir, vs. a Parshall flume.
- Are you using water in an area that is water stressed or water abundant? Does this matter to you (the answer to this one should always be "yes"!)? Do you even know how to find out?
- What about the quality of the water? Are you polluting the groundwater or surface water bodies with your discharge? Would you even know where and how to find out?
- How does the local community feel about your company's use of the water sources?

I think you get the idea. These are only a handful of the hundreds of questions that can be asked about something as seemingly simple as water use. Now, imagine how many other "non-financial metrics" could be of interest in the sustainability space, and the collective variables and questions associated with each of them! This relates also to the chapter in which I described the concept of "social investment" vs. "philanthropy," and how you quantitate the softer return on investment in the social development space. This can quickly leave the boundaries of a company's expertise or core capability. After all, most companies know how to measure and report finances... but how do you measure and report how effective you were at developing a community? How do you quantitate and articulate the impact you've had on education? Literacy rates? Farm yield and farmer income? Access to cell phones and internet? It's not easy. So, what do you do?

The answer may sound pat, and is not intended to sound evasive...but you do what makes sense for your business to do...and you MUST do it TRANSPARENTLY. What does "transparency" mean? There are several good attempts to define what transparency means for business, especially in the context of the development, selection, and reporting of sustainability metrics, and these can be found on my website, www.danbena.com.

I personally think that "transparency" is a spectrum—a continuum—where there is always room for improvement. In a nutshell, I suggest that these three elements are critical to transparent reporting:

1. Accuracy and precision. The expectation is that

you will do your best to report numbers that are both accurate and precise. The magician's trick of pulling a number out of a hat definitely has no place in the reporting of non-financial metrics (or financial, for that matter).

2. Honesty and candor. This is sometimes the hardest part of truly transparent reporting, because it is always easier to tell the good news. Transparency, however, requires that you tell the bad news, as well. It's great to establish a goal and report progress toward reaching it, but the reality is that there are some goals that will not be met in the time frame allowed. In these cases, you mustn't just extend the time frame! You need to communicate that you will not meet the goal, why, and what you are planning to do to meet it in the future.

3. Line of sight to the horizon. This is related to number two, but also includes sharing what the "big picture" is with your stakeholders and interested parties. Of course, you wouldn't want to disclose something that is proprietary or confidential from a competitive business perspective, but it is a great stride along the transparency continuum to report your short-, medium-, and long-term goals and plans. How does what you are reporting in one year relate to what was reported in previous years? How

does it relate to what you hope to report in future years?

I struggled with whether to include a fourth element of transparency: external verification or assurance of the numbers being reported. This is becoming an increasingly important step in the evolution of transparent reporting. Here again, there are many consulting companies available to assist in these efforts, and they vary in their rigor, approach, and cost. Typically, there is a distinction between assurance and verification, with the latter usually being more comprehensive, and therefore more costly. The concept, however, is a good one in the eyes of many external stakeholders..."trust but verify." Yours could be the greatest company in the world, adored by your consumers, but they still would likely have a bit more confidence in numbers if they were verified by an independent third party, vs. numbers that were only self-reported. It's human nature to large extent, and something which must be figured in, eventually, to a company's overall sustainability strategy. As you might imagine, the numbers for some things are much more easily verified than for others. For example, something like electricity usage should be easy, either tracked directly from a meter (assuming the meter is routinely calibrated), or tracked indirectly through bills from the electric utility. Similarly, water usage, fuel usage, employee injury rates, financial losses due to significant incidents—all are relatively easy to measure. As long as the systems are in place to manage the metrics and the people responsible for collecting and reporting the metrics are capable, third parties should look favorably upon these kinds of straightforward metrics.

Now, consider for a moment collecting and assuring metrics that are not so straightforward, those that don't lend themselves to easy quantification. For example, what if you own a company, and your consumers are interested in any human rights abuses to the day laborers on farms in developing countries that you do not own, but with whom you contract? What if they want to know the impact of your water use? Not how much you use, but the impact of that use on the community. What if you are a detergent manufacturer and your influential investors are insisting on knowing the levels of some esoteric metal contaminant that might occur in one or more of your raw materials which you source from a developing country with little to no analytic monitoring capability? You get the idea. These examples, though they may sound contrived, are very much within the realm of real expectations of the "socially responsible" company.

Remember in one of the earlier chapters, I talked about the recurring theme of "balance"? It applies to this topic, especially. You must balance carefully where you plan to focus your efforts, and how.

Key Take-Aways from Chapter Four

1. You motivate a politician to act by getting his/her constituents to align on a common message. You motivate a company to act by understanding what its consumers want. It is worth spending money to collect these data.

2. Consumers across much of the world hold companies responsible for three things: protecting the planet, treating people fairly, and providing safe and high quality products. These should form the mantra of any good sustainability strategy.

3. Consumers aren't the only stakeholders, but are important ones. Companies need to identify and map their most important stakeholder groups, including the "influencers," and then develop clear strategies to engage each category.

4. Goals, and credible metrics to track them, are essential.

5. Transparency in reporting is non-negotiable. It requires accuracy and precision of the metrics, candor and honesty in reporting, and providing the context of where things fit into the overall strategy. Third party assurance of non-financial metrics is becoming an increasing expectation, so it is best to comply sooner rather than later.

5

Will Sustainability Survive Challenging Macroeconomic Times?

A fair question...and one I will answer in two ways. The first is what I think the answer SHOULD be, and the second is the reality of what the answer really is. I'm not doing this merely to indulge myself with the reading audience...there is a point to these two responses.

The first answer was conveyed by a speaker at the Clinton Global Initiative meeting in New York City in late 2008, and several thought leaders in this space have espoused and communicated it since. It relates to the old adage, "when the going gets tough, the tough get going." In other words, when the going gets tough, which is when people really need the positive impact of sustainable development, is when companies—and governments—and anyone who gives a darn—should *accelerate* their efforts, not diminish them. Think about it—and think about it in the context of the current unprecedented macroeconomic challenges with which the country and the world are faced. Rampant unemployment, poverty, homelessness…isn't this PRECISELY the time when people need help? It sounds so intuitive, right? This is when the proverbial "rubber hits the road." It's easy to be generous when times are good, but our mettle is tested when times are hard. This is true of companies, governments, and individuals…in fact, it is true of everyone. Although I am not old enough to have endured the challenges of the Great Depression, the concept in this chapter reminds me of a song (1931) by Harburg and Gorney which was popular during that time in America's history. "Once I built a tower, up to the sun, brick, and rivet, and lime; Once I built a tower, now it's done. Brother, can you spare a dime?"

The idea of building the tower can be likened to building an economy and developing society, only to have this progress end—and end abruptly--leaving as destitute people who were once thriving, contributing members of the society they helped build. The problem was that many family members, friends, and neighbors were also destitute—a pan-national economic crisis—so everyone was suffering together. Yet, despite this crippling financial turmoil, the song asks, "Brother, can you spare a dime?" The most remarkable thing, which is so germane to the message of this chapter, is that many did, indeed, spare that dime. Although they didn't really have it to spare, they did—they shared it with their fellow brethren, many of whom were complete strangers. The bond was their adversity.

The bond was their adversity...worth a second thought, and maybe even a third, since it is a powerful insight into human nature. As violently competitive and territorial as people can be, wanting to protect what is theirs, an interesting thing happens when common adversity—significant adversity—strikes: people unite.

The lyrics of "building a tower" can't help but make me think back to the horrific events that razed the Twin Towers of the World Trade Center in New York City on September 11, 2001. Whether you are a conspiracy theorist, an avid soldier against the "war on terror," or a political zealot matters not in this context. What matters is what happened the morning of the catastrophe—and what remained for months (some might argue even years) afterward. People united. Within seconds, people of all races, colors, creeds, gender, sexual orientation, political beliefs—whatever—UNITED to help each other. They didn't scramble to take care of themselves, or rush to protect what was personally theirs. They banded together—immediately—to help others. We need to somehow capture the positive part of this phenomenon, and replicate it—replicate it across the world. Wouldn't it be great if people across the world felt this sense of unity for humanity EVERY DAY, without the need for a common catastrophe to spark it?

Bringing this back to the first answer to the question posed at the beginning of this chapter, "Will sustainability survive challenging economic times?" I would argue that the answer is, "it must." Period.

Unfortunately, I can't just leave the topic so simply, because, to a certain extent, that answer looks through the lens of those proverbial "rose-colored glasses"...perhaps a bit more optimistic—or hopeful--than realistic. On a corporate level, especially for companies that are publicly traded, the primary responsibility is to the shareholders. These shareholders generally expect a healthy return of earnings per share, which is usually why they bought the company's stock in the first place...to make money. And moneymaking through sound investments is not a "dirty word"; not a desire of which to be ashamed, even in sustainability circles! As a result, though, the leadership of the company, and its Board, are normally very diligent about how much money the company spends, and how.

Now, I wish that I could report to you that everyone sees the innate link of sustainability to direct profitability of the business, but this is simply not the case. It continues to be a long, often taxing, battle to convince people that sustainability is more than philanthropy. It's more than a pot of money you set aside to use to write checks to charities during times of natural disaster. It is not a *part* of the business, or something that sits *aside* the business; sustainability *is* the business...or at least it should be. Recall in an earlier chapter, I mentioned that business is "A PART OF" the community" and does not sit "APART FROM" it? Same concept here. If you truly believe this, and comprehend its many facets, then you are truly enlightened, and you would absolutely understand a company that accelerates its sustainability efforts when "the going gets tough." Many companies, though, are at a different point in their journey. Their leadership would very likely nod their heads at the concepts presented in this chapter, and say that they make sense (and I think many would believe this), but when push comes to shove, and they are asked to approve funding for a social investment during a difficult financial period, the money would not come forth. Sad, but true.

In the case of the current economic challenges, the story really is quite mixed. There are many companies that have significantly decreased their "sustainability" spending, including even that which would be considered traditional philanthropy. There are others, however, who managed to strike an equitable balance in order to help them navigate the financial head- and tail-winds. Many have continued to support existing partnerships, but have either decreased or ceased additional funding of these or new efforts, pending the eventual economic upswing. Don't misunderstand me—and I want to be very clear—companies are NOT non-profits. They are entities whose shared objective is to make money. For public companies, they must additionally return value to their shareholders in the form of healthy returns. With this premise, of course, the company cannot afford to fund so many sustainability initiatives that their financial health is poor. This is not what I am suggesting at all. However, consider that even in difficult economic times, there are still creative ways in which companies can contribute to community—beyond money. The more diligent—and, I dare say, visionary—companies have actually increased their social investments, whether through direct spending, provision of *pro bono* services, capability sharing, product promotions and discounts, or through many other innovative approaches.

As with life, the best solution is usually not at either end of a spectrum—it lies somewhere in the middle. Remember, another common message in this book, which I mentioned before—the natural order is one of balance, not existing at either pole of a wide spectrum. This is also true for the fate of sustainability in the wake of severe economic turmoil. Companies must choose a middle ground, one which makes sense for their individual culture and business, one which will resonate with their shareholders, consumers, and other interested stakeholders. Irrespective of which path is chosen, it remains critically important that the path itself be communicated... transparently (as discussed in chapter four).

Key Take-Aways from Chapter Five

1. The comprehensive business case for sustainability is often not intuitive to many senior leaders. As a result, the common "burning platform" is often cost savings through productivity.

2. In challenging economic times, if you can't justify sustainability-related spending by an acceptable return on investment (traditional financial ROI), the spending will often not be approved. In these cases, patience is the key.

3. Companies are not non-profits. They are intended to make money, and this is a good thing. The key is to discover ways to make money while still contributing positively to society.

4. The reality, which truly enlightened companies understand, is that it is precisely during times of difficult economics that you should increase your investment in sustainability...not scale it back. Sustainable development is not something that sits aside from the business—it IS the business. It is the only reliable method to assure that the business thrives long-term...and sustainably.

6

Performance with Purpose: The PepsiCo Model for Sustainability in Action

"Performance with Purpose." Think about this for few seconds. What does it mean? Is it intuitive to you as a reader? "Performance" can mean a lot of things, surely, but to most, if not all, businesses, "performance" refers at least in part to the financial performance of the company. Think of it as the way Wall Street and the financial media would report on the progress of the company—things like earnings per share, price to earnings ratios, and other indicators as to the financial "fitness" of the company.

Remember, though, that in an earlier chapter, I talked at length about the "triple bottom line" and that now-a-days, financial "performance" is only one piece of the puzzle—admittedly an important one. To complement this, however, there are also societal and environmental expectations of "performance."

In this section I will discuss my experience with, and perspective of, the sustainability efforts at my employer, PepsiCo. However, before going further, I need to emphasize that the following statements, observations and comments are mine alone. They do not reflect or represent any policy, stance, aspiration, goal, initiative, etc., of PepsiCo, and my statements, observations and comments are being made by me as an individual, and not as an employee or representative of PepsiCo. There—now I got the Legal disclaimer out of the way!!

At PepsiCo, the company has stated that its performance—financial, environmental, and societal—is and must be driven by "purpose." Hence the combination of "Performance with Purpose." The term was coined by PepsiCo's Chair and CEO Indra K. Nooyi, and was introduced at a meeting of the American Chambers of Commerce in India in late 2006. Since then, the term has resonated, especially with the company's nearly 300,000 employees across the world. It has provided PepsiCo associates around the world with a banner and a rallying cry around which to organize their efforts related to sustainable development. But "Performance with Purpose" is so much more than just a rallying cry. It is a way to embed sustainable development into the "corporate DNA"—to assure that it is not merely the flavor of the month, but that it is genuinely a long-term approach to assure that the business, the communities served by the business, and broader society develop and thrive for years to come. Let's take a closer look at the elements of Performance with Purpose as it is applied across PepsiCo.

Performance with Purpose has three main planks: Human Sustainability, Talent Sustainability, and Environmental Sustainability. Human Sustainability refers to the products the company provides to consumers in nearly 200 countries around the world. It means a lot to a food and beverage company that millions of consumers trust the brand enough to eat and drink the company's products, so PepsiCo believes it has an obligation—a responsibility—to make sure that these products are safe and refreshing. The company takes this responsibility very seriously, which is why it is undertaking to transform its product portfolio to include more products that better nourish its consumers. One of the refreshing things about PepsiCo is that, from its Chair and CEO down to the line workers, it is very clear about its identity. It is a company that provides great tasting and refreshing treats to consumers around the world. There will always be a balanced mix of some products that are "fun for you"—like the company's flagship brands, Pepsi-Cola or Lays potato chips—and some products that provide other types of nutrition—including those containing more fiber, protein, nuts and seeds, and juices.

Talent Sustainability is the plank of Performance with Purpose that refers to the company's employees--the talent the company has currently and the talent the company expects to attract and retain for years to come. This is critically linked to society, since people who are happy, rewarded, and fulfilled at work often are highly engaged people—socially conscious and contributing members of society. This plank of Performance with Purpose also includes an important goal—treating every single one of the company's associates, all over the world, with respect and fairness according to the PepsiCo values and code of conduct. This includes the company striving to keep its employees intellectually challenged, professionally supported, and physically healthy and safe at work and at home.

The third plank of Performance with Purpose is likely the most intuitive—Environmental Sustainability. As the name implies, this plank refers to the company's overall environmental stewardship—and also to how this applies to the triple bottom line to which I have referred several times in this book. It forms the guiding foundation for many of PepsiCo's efforts. PepsiCo's Environmental Sustainability plank includes critical core focus areas— water (from perspectives of both quality and quantity), climate change (energy use, greenhouse gases), and land (packaging, solid waste, and sustainable agriculture).

As you hopefully already read in the Forward of this book, this year marks my 25th year with PepsiCo, and the company has helped me find my passion—which is, in fact, sustainable development—by leveraging PepsiCo's resources, reach, and influence to positively impact the world. So, from that perspective, I am admittedly biased, but PepsiCo is a great company that has done—and continues to do—a lot of great things. It's more than just "lip service" to make the company look good externally; it is working to catalyze real progress in the world, whether it's in health and nutrition, inspirational leadership, or helping to tackle the many global environmental crises with which the world is faced. This book, though, is not meant to be an advertisement for PepsiCo. I do urge the reader to learn more about the company's sustainable development efforts on its public website, *www.pepsico.com*. You will likely be surprised (and pleasantly), but definitely impressed!

This chapter is less about the great things PepsiCo is doing, and more about how the company ended up where it is today. After all, the book is intended to help companies develop, evolve, and enrich their own strategy for sustainable development, and no two companies will have the exact same approach. What will be common, though, and what is translatable, are the rationale and journey.

"Journey" is an interesting concept—and one which has been used a lot in this context. Many companies talk about their "sustainability journey," in large part because it really is—a journey. It is not an initiative that has well-defined start and end times, and is something that businesses must realize the importance of being in for the long haul! It is a multi-year—perhaps decades-long—journey, with many incremental achievements along the way.

PepsiCo's sustainability journey has been credited with having been started in 1999, which is when Frito-Lay, one of PepsiCo's businesses, established environmental metrics and goals to track. In reality, PepsiCo has been engaged in sustainable development—true sustainable development—for decades. My long-time friend and mentor, Harry DeLonge, would regale me with anecdotes from back in the 1960s and 70s of how the company's international businesses thought creatively to reach out to the communities around the company's manufacturing plants. Two such stories that he shared—and he was personally leading them at the time—involved providing one of PepsiCo's plant waste streams to swine farmers in China and sharing capability with tilapia fish farmers in the Philippines. In the China example, the PepsiCo plant water treatment stream, while perfectly acceptable for discharge, was mixed with swine feed, and resulted in fatter swine, which improved yield...so the farmers had more to sell...and, therefore, made more money. Economic development. The Philippines example was an early case study of how a company can share capability—not always money—with people in communities that need it. PepsiCo has some of the best water treatment technologists in the world working in its plants. In the Philippines, as Harry relates it, the company shared this expertise with the fish farmers to improve the water quality and treatment they used to grow their tilapia, and also increased the yield and quality of their fish! Both stories, admittedly without hard metrics 40 years ago, were examples of sustainable development in practice—but it wasn't called "sustainable development" at the time. In fact, these activities far pre-dated the Brundtland report which helped formalize and expand awareness of sustainable development. They also were being actively engaged long before the UN Millennium Development Goals were even a concept! At the time, it was, simply put, good business; the community was happy, and the company was happy. That's the concept in a nut shell.

When PepsiCo's Chair and CEO introduced the term and concept of "Performance with Purpose" in late 2006, it was, in many ways, the "shot heard 'round the world"— at least within the PepsiCo world! It almost immediately provided a tangible banner—an umbrella under which all of the sustainability efforts with which the company had been involved could be grouped, and linked, and leveraged for genuine collective impact. Never under-estimate the value of words—or of a catchy "tag line."

Marketing? *Maybe.* Motivating? *Definitely.*

This single change marked the beginning of a real evolution at PepsiCo. The company went from having a collection of worthwhile, but admittedly *ad hoc* and often disparate initiatives, to being given the "permission" to develop a strong, cohesive, unified sustainable development strategy and action for PepsiCo. And this "permission" was led from the proverbial "top down." Many companies may consider it a luxury to have a CEO championing these efforts. Often, sustainability practitioners will find themselves building a compelling business case—the so called "burning platform"—to engage their senior leaders, in an attempt to catalyze action. In PepsiCo's case, its CEO—having grown up in a developing economy and having witnessed many societal challenges—was already "there." She "got it." So, from that perspective, the jobs of PepsiCo associates charged with advancing sustainable development were made that much simpler.

I must quickly point out, however, that this wasn't the end of it! In addition to her passion for the company's laudable sustainability efforts, PepsiCo's CEO was formerly the company's Chief Financial Officer (CFO), so she understands the traditional value of "performance" better than anyone. This underscored the need to balance the "purpose" the company embraces with assuring sound and consistent value to its shareholders. This is not always an easy balance to strike, and the company's Chair and CEO continues today to challenge all associates to be sure that they are, indeed, striking that balance.

So, clearly, top-down support helps—and helps a great deal. But so do "grass roots" efforts, which were occurring simultaneously to the formal architecture being developed at PepsiCo's senior levels. Employees in the company's manufacturing facilities and offices around the world also seemed to be increasing their awareness of sustainability—in particular, environmental sustainability, since this seems to resonate with the broadest audiences most of all. It seems to make intuitive sense that if the planet fails, so does everything else. Examples began to pop up from around the enterprise, from the formation of volunteer "green teams" of passionate employees from across multiple functions at Frito Lay plants to teams of dedicated associates beginning robust office recycling initiatives to collect office waste and track the number of trees saved at Walkers in the United Kingdom and Gamesa in Mexico. Pockets of employees volunteered to clean up rivers and streams on their days off, and junior associates catalyzed campaigns to replace incandescent light bulbs with compact fluorescents and use ceramic mugs instead of disposable coffee cups! These grass roots movements took the company by storm, and continue today. Sparking the interest and passion of employees is one of a company's most powerful assets.

Great. So now the company has a name for its sustainable development operating model, a rallying cry, focus areas, top-down support, and a variety of grass-roots efforts bubbling up from across the world. Now what? Leverage and "connect the dots."

It is almost unavoidable that as a company embarks on its sustainable development journey, there will emerge a number of seemingly disparate, unconnected projects. These projects tend to follow peoples' passions or personal experiences. If, for example, someone is a devoted member of Rotary International, or some other community group or NGO, it is likely that they will bring that "cause" to their business efforts. As tempting as this is, it would be best in the long run to systematically and strategically assess these potential initiatives, and only focus on the ones that are the right "fit" for the business plans. For example, PepsiCo was funding several projects over the years in many geographies that were laudable, but not firmly connected to the company's evolving Performance with Purpose operating model and focus areas. So, over time, the company transitioned from these projects to projects which seemed to be a better "fit" for PepsiCo's strategy. Engaging in a project for a project's sake may not be the best way to effect change…the driving objective should be impact. The best and most efficient way to achieve impact is to make sure that all of your sustainability efforts across the company and across the world are in some way connected. They need to be complementary and, ideally (although this is an often over-used word in corporate speak), "synergistic." That is, the impact of the collective efforts ideally should be greater than the additive impact of each individual effort on its own.

When PepsiCo arrived at a point in its journey at which it was beginning to have impact—real, significant impact—the company quickly realized the importance of communication and engagement—on all levels. It is critically important for a company to tell its story, and tell it both internally and externally...but be warned. When you begin to communicate more decidedly internally, be prepared for a veritable ground swell of employee interest and passion. You must be prepared to harness and direct that passion, or else it can quickly fizzle, and may be very difficult to re-ignite! When you begin to communicate more strategically externally, be aware that anecdote alone—no matter how great the story--is no longer adequate. Robust, quantifiable, and verifiable metrics are the clear expectation of many stakeholder groups, so be prepared. Chapter Four covers this concept of transparency in much more detail. In addition, the reality is that no matter how great you might think your company's sustainability achievements are, there will always be groups with other agendas that will be highly critical of your efforts. While this can be daunting, it should not deflate the momentum to continue to make positive progress for the business, the communities you serve, and greater society. Stay strong and focused!

Back to Performance with Purpose, and the continuing journey at PepsiCo. One of the more crucial things with which to end this section is this: you must be ready—and accept this as fact—for your sustainable development strategy to be a dynamic, changing entity. You must be willing to accept change—even embrace it—and amend your strategy and your actions to suit the needs of your business and your stakeholders. I just recently sat on a panel at the World Bank in Washington, DC that was all about "adaptation"—how societies, governments, even individuals, need to be flexible enough to adapt to the changing global and local environments around them. This is also true of businesses. The business that is successful long-term will be the one that recognizes the possible challenges in the future, and is nimble enough to change to address them…turning proverbial "risks" into genuine "opportunities." You can learn more about the details of Performance with Purpose, as PepsiCo continues to increase the robustness and transparency of the company's reporting each year, by visiting *www.pepsico.com*.

At PepsiCo, the company's passionate employees have been on this journey of sustainable development for years—or decades—depending on where you place the "start" mark, and one thing is sure: they quickly recognize that they will be on it for many years to come.

Key Take-Aways from Chapter Six

1. As pat as it may sound, you must recognize that sustainable development—for societies, governments, individuals, or companies—is a journey, a long journey, years or decades in the making. The important thing is to *start* on the journey.

2. As much as possible, choose focus areas that are a good "fit" for your business and for the strategic approach you have developed for the business. There are many worthwhile "causes" in the world, but not all of them will complement your business.

3. When you have selected the focus areas and momentum is building across your organization, take the time and diligence to harness that momentum. That is, "connect the dots" across your business to be sure that multiple projects are complementary and connected.

4. Let impact be the driver. Measure the impact. Report the impact routinely, accurately, and transparently.

7

Where Should Companies Begin On Their Sustainability Journey?

As a scientist at heart, the question posed above had me torn as I considered how to address it and provide the best guidance. When we first met, my mentor, Harry DeLonge (mentioned earlier in this book), had one major complaint about me (it might have been presented as "constructive feedback" at the time, but you get the point). It was that I was "too buttoned up." I would receive a question from one of my internal customers, perhaps from across the world (via telex at the time—long before email was invented), and I would immediately begin to work on an answer—for days, or sometimes weeks. I would want to make sure that every proverbial "i" was dotted and every "t" was crossed. After all, I wanted to provide the most robust and comprehensive reply possible to the person that had asked the question. In the interim, the requestor would have no idea what I was doing. They were not part of the process, really; only to the extent that they posed a question, and then received an answer. Harry imparted one of the most useful pearls of wisdom I have ever received: "You don't always have to be completely buttoned up," Harry said. "Make people part of the process. They are much more appreciative if they are part of the solution from the beginning." Sage advice, for sure, and applicable to this chapter.

The start of any sustainability journey should be engagement—dialog—to make people part of the process. Depending on the size of the company and the empowerment of the people leading the effort, this engagement could take many forms: Maybe a talk with the CEO or Board of Directors, or maybe just your immediate manager, the line employees, or office staff...or maybe all of these, and more! You need to acquire some foundational information, which I will call the "Five Gems"—because there is real value in understanding and acting on these gems:

- What is the level of knowledge / familiarity of people in your business with the concepts of sustainable development. These concepts are usually easy to teach in a short period of time.

- *Knowledge* is one thing, but *belief* is another. Maybe they have the knowledge, but do they *believe* in the power of a sustainability program? As you might expect, this is much more difficult to "teach." Some people never get it, but it is great—transformative—when they do!

- What is your business's core expertise, and how does it relate to possible focus areas for your sustainable development journey? For example, if your company makes "high-end" cowhide leather purses targeted at women, you might consider focusing on how the cows are treated—are they humanely euthanized? Are the hides the by-product of cows that are grown for food, or are they grown specifically for the hides? Knowing where to focus is VERY important for the journey. The water used to raise the cows, while it may be significant, is probably not the place to start.

- Who are your most important stakeholders, and why? This is a very valuable question to address early on, because it helps formalize your thought processes and informs your focus areas, initiative selections, and messaging later on. Construct a "stakeholder map" to identify who has a vested interest in what your company does. Governments—local, national, international? Investors? Employees? NGOs? Faith-based groups? Academia? Media? Others?

- What do the stakeholders care about? Knowing your stakeholders is important, for sure, but engaging them to find out what they care about is even more critical. Sometimes, it's not easy, because you may not want to hear their message…it may cause added complexity for your business or highlight an issue which you have not previously addressed "head on." Believe me, it will benefit you in the long run to engage stakeholders at the beginning for a candid dialog. The one caveat to this, of course, as we addressed in a previous chapter, is that the stakeholders be receptive, even if minimally so. They should be willing to open the door to dialog—if only a crack!

These don't necessarily have to be performed in any particular sequence, but they usually follow a logical progression once you begin the journey. One dialog leads to another, and so on and so on. That said, the first two above are quite important to assess as early on as possible. It's usually exponentially easier if your CEO or company owner "gets it" and understands the value of a sustainable development journey and program, but there are other ways to build momentum, as well. You can catalyze a ground swell from the "bottom up." Usually, if enough employees are passionate and engaged in an effort, even the most reticent or stubborn CEO will eventually stand up and take notice. And when this happens, it represents a valuable educational and awareness-building opportunity.

The other way to build momentum is to get the proverbial "foot in the door." That is, if you get some "quick wins" under your belt—wins that save money—that's another way to capture senior leadership attention. While they may not know about or fully understand "sustainable development," I guarantee they will understand productivity savings. This is typical early on in a sustainability journey, since virtually all businesses today use natural resources—either water, fuel, electricity, land, or all of them. Consequently, most businesses can usually save a significant amount of money in the first few years by measuring their use and taking steps to reduce it. It's astounding what the mere process of measurement can do to control something. If you don't routinely measure your resource use, what reliable way do you have to reduce it? Once you save your company money through these eco-efficiency or productivity interventions, it is amazing how much credibility you gain in the eyes of your company leadership, which makes for a much more receptive audience to expand the "eco-efficiency" dialog to one that includes "sustainability," and then "sustainable development"!

One way or another, you need to establish the "business case" for sustainability. These business cases can take a variety of forms, and the details will often vary with the business, sector, leadership team, and other factors. One business case was already discussed above— financial savings through eco-efficiency improvements. This is often the easiest, because when a company first begins its sustainability plan, there is a lot of "low hanging fruit"—things which are easy to positively impact. Things like changing from incandescent to compact fluorescent bulbs, utilizing flow regulators on sinks, low-flow toilets, double-sided printing...simple things which easily can be found with a few diligent Google searches. The other business case, as discussed in chapter four, especially for consumer products companies, is to understand and communicate what your consumers want. This is the quickest way to assure continued success of the business—give your consumers what they want. Increasingly, consumers across the globe "want" sustainability—whether this means "green" products and services, social responsibility, "smart philanthropy," or "fair trade" sourcing—the message is clear: this matters to consumers, and matters enough to affect their purchasing decisions. A powerful "business case," indeed.

One of the equally (or more) powerful business cases, but one which is much more difficult to explain (and nearly impossible today to quantitate with precision), is the power of preserving the "license to operate." Here, again, this can mean literally the life or death of the business. In large part, the company doesn't own its license to operate; it is granted by their stakeholders—and is often (almost continuously) up for renewal. You need to earn and re-earn your company's license to operate through actions and impact. Unfortunately, many businesses only learn of the power of this license when they lose it, at which point it is much more difficult to re-gain (sometimes, it expires forever!). The smartest companies—and hopefully as a reader you will belong to one of them—are those who understand the value of this license to operate *proactively*—before it is lost.

Many other elements can be included in developing a business case; in fact, a robust and compelling one *will* incorporate multiple considerations. For example, if your company is publicly traded, investors and shareholders have a very important voice in shaping the direction your company takes. They, too, are increasingly interested in sustainability, and from a purely logical perspective— minimizing business risks. They realize that it has become a substantive risk to most businesses to ignore sustainable development—including all three elements of the "triple bottom line" (social, economic, and environmental, as discussed in Chapter One). Many are only now investing in companies that do far more than "not ignore" sustainability—those that embrace it and embed it into their business strategic and daily processes. One of the best white papers I have seen on the topic of business risks and opportunities posed by sustainable development was created by a group of investors and other stakeholders, called Ceres. It systematically characterizes the risks and opportunities for businesses across multiple sectors, and lists very tangible steps business can (and must) take to mitigate these risks and maximize these opportunities. The report from February 2009 is entitled, "Water Scarcity and Climate Change: Growing Risks for Businesses and Investors," and is available on their website, www.ceres.org. In addition to the Ceres report, one other treatise, specific to business, was published by the World Business Council for Sustainable Development (WBCSD). In this report, the opportunities for business to enable and catalyze adaptation to the myriad climate crises are thoughtfully and informatively addressed. This report, entitled, "Adaptation: An Issue Brief for Business," may be downloaded from their website at www.wbcsd. org. For companies anywhere along the road of their sustainability journey, these two documents should be considered "must read" resources.

Key Take-Aways from Chapter Seven

1. Start on the journey. Don't wait to be "buttoned up."

2. Make people part of the process.

3. Ascertain the level of knowledge of sustainability in your company, and how much people really believe in it.

4. Understand your business's core expertise, and construct your sustainability plan to leverage and complement it.

5. Map your stakeholders and understand why they are important.

6. Engage with your stakeholders to understand what they want from you.

8

Closing Messages From the Author: The Critical "Take Aways"

For me, this is the easy part. All I have to do is copy the "critical take aways" from the end of each chapter to make it easier with them all located in one place. This way, if you want to print them or copy them to refer to, you don't have to page through the entire book! Your job, on the other hand, is just beginning. You need to take what you've read, digest it, augment it, understand it, and then implement it! No matter where you end up, the journey itself really is the fun part, and I have no doubt that you, your company, your families, and friends will be better off because you took the step toward embracing sustainable development. It's good for the "three Ps"—people, planet, and profit!

Key Take-Aways from Chapter One

1. The Triple Bottom Line is a model based on the traditional concept of the financial bottom line and was devised to help quantitatively compare companies among their peers and competitors.

2. The Triple Bottom Line expands what is expected in the definition of a "profitable business" to include not only the financial performance and how it contributes to economy, but also the softer side of performance: how a company contributes to society and helps protect the environment.

3. Different models exist that paint the elements of the triple bottom line—society, economy, and environment--with an equal brush, but recognize that if the planet fails, society and economy cease to exist.

4. The triple bottom line is more than a model on a piece of paper. It is—or can be—a very valuable concept for how businesses should conduct their day-to-day activities to assure success for decades to come.

Key Take-Aways from Chapter Two

1. The difference between the terms "sustainability" and "sustainable development" is more than just semantics.

2. "Sustainability" is used more often by people from private industry, and implies the sustainability of their business which will result from funding and leading societal and environmental initiatives.

3. "Sustainable Development" is used more often by people from non-profit entities and other non-government organizations, and places the development of society and protection of environment as paramount. Positive benefits to business will be secondary, and a direct result of societal and environmental efforts.

Key Take-Aways from Chapter Three

1. There are many points along the Purpose Spectrum at which companies can activate their corporate responsibility programs. Striking the proper balance between traditional philanthropy and business funding is key.

2. In the US and other countries, funding by a corporate Foundation **is strictly regulated by tax law**. You must understand these laws completely, and interpret them in a way that allows Foundation strategies to *complement* the strategies of the business.

3. Finding ways to calculate an ROI for social investments, just as businesses would calculate an ROI for financial investments, is critical to accelerate the acceptance and success of corporate responsibility programs.

4. Front running companies are those that have already heeded the advice of my colleague: "CSR cannot be seen as something *additional* to the business; it must be seen as something that *is* the business."

5. To "do" sustainability properly, as with anything, companies need a structure to manage it and the resources to support it. The structure could range from a lean central function headed by a Chief Sustainability Officer, to cross-business, interconnected Committees or Councils to provide the needed thought leadership to the business. Many architectures can be effective, but it depends on the goals, focus areas, and objectives of the function.

Key Take-Aways from Chapter Four

1. You motivate a politician to act by getting his/her constituents to align on a common message. You motivate a company to act by understanding what its consumers want. It is worth spending money to collect these data.

2. Consumers across much of the world hold companies responsible for three things: protecting the planet, treating people fairly, and providing safe and high quality products. These should form the mantra of any good sustainability strategy.

3. Consumers aren't the only stakeholders, but are important ones. Companies need to identify and map their most important stakeholder groups, including the "influencers," and then develop clear strategies to engage each category.

4. Goals, and credible metrics to track them, are essential.

5. Transparency in reporting is non-negotiable. It requires accuracy and precision of the metrics, candor and honesty in reporting, and providing the context of where things fit into the overall strategy. Third party assurance of non-financial metrics is becoming an increasing expectation, so it is best to comply sooner rather than later.

Key Take-Aways from Chapter Five

1. The comprehensive business case for sustainability is often not intuitive to many senior leaders. As a result, the common "burning platform" is often cost savings through productivity.

2. In challenging economic times, if you can't justify sustainability-related spending by an acceptable return on investment (traditional financial ROI), the spending will often not be approved. In these cases, patience is the key.

3. Companies are not non-profits. They are intended to make money, and this is a good thing. The key is to discover ways to make money while still contributing positively to society.

4. The reality, which truly enlightened companies understand, is that it is precisely during times of difficult economics that you should increase your investment in sustainability...not scale it back. Sustainable development is not something that sits aside from the business—it IS the business. It is the only reliable method to assure that the business thrives long-term...and sustainably.

Key Take-Aways from Chapter Six

1. As pat as it may sound, you must recognize that sustainable development—for societies, governments, individuals, or companies—is a journey, a long journey, years or decades in the making. The important thing is to *start* on the journey.

2. As much as possible, choose focus areas that are a good "fit" for your business and for the strategic approach you have developed for the business. There are many worthwhile "causes" in the world, but not all of them will complement your business.

3. When you have selected the focus areas and momentum is building across your organization, take the time and diligence to harness that momentum. That is, "connect the dots" across your business to be sure that multiple projects are complementary and connected.

4. Let impact be the driver. Measure the impact. Report the impact routinely and transparently.

Key Take-Aways from Chapter Seven

1. Start on the journey. Don't wait to be "buttoned up."

2. Make people part of the process.

3. Ascertain the level of knowledge of sustainability in your company, and how much people really believe in it.

4. Understand your business's core expertise, and construct your sustainability plan to leverage and complement it.

5. Map your stakeholders and understand why they are important.

6. Engage with your stakeholders to understand what they want from you.

9

A Quarter-Century Of Lessons Learned—For The Price Of The Book!

This chapter of the book might be a little less traditional than the chapters in many books intended for the professional corporate audience. Less traditional because it isn't really specifically about the title of the book, which is sustainability. It's more about the author, me, sharing many experiences with the reader—experiences which I hope will be helpful. As I write this, I am sitting at a desk overlooking the Atlantic Ocean, at a gorgeous, completely renovated, turn-of-the century beach resort in Watch Hill, Rhode Island. What does my presence at the Ocean House have to do with the chapter of this book?

The reason I am here is because I am with my wife, for a brief escape to celebrate 24 years of wedded bliss—and it really is wedded bliss. Positive karma has really smiled upon me by placing my wife in my path nearly 30 years ago—but why should you care? The 24 years of marriage went by in what felt like an instant! Truly, people sometimes refer to their wedding anniversary sarcastically when they say with a bit of a wry look, "it seemed like yesterday." I genuinely mean it.

While my wife is painting the ocean view, I would like to take the time to complete what will be the final chapter in this book. What better way in which to frame "lessons learned" than to think back on a quarter of a century—what worked, what didn't, what I wish had worked, and what I wish hadn't? So you, as a reader, have been great in indulging me—my tangents—my diversions—but I hope they have proven to be more than just disjointed, or irrelevant. I hope you realized that they were done—each and every one—strategically, either to highlight a message that I believe is important with a bit of color commentary, or to subliminally convey an equally important, though less direct, message. This chapter, too, is intended to help you, by learning from my mistakes, as well as my successes. You can, perhaps, do the "mistakes" differently, and have them work, or repeat the successes, and make them better.

I think back to when I began at PepsiCo—a laboratory technician who was in the Teamsters' Union—yes, me, a Teamster. No one in my family would have seen that coming, and I was so naïve right out of college that I had no idea of the implications—both good and bad. All I knew at the time was that the job with PepsiCo was paying more than the job I was offered to be a morgue attendant, and it seemed to be a lot "cleaner" work, so I took it. On my hiring day, the Human Resources representative told, "You realize that this is a Union position...." Made no difference to me. "Yes," I said sheepishly...and me, so began my career with PepsiCo.

The years in the Teamsters' Union were some of the most enlightening of my life, especially for a young graduate just out of college with a bit of a chip on his shoulder, thinking that his Bachelor's degree in Biochemistry was the be-all, end-all! I had a lot to learn...and learn I did. The Teamsters folks really didn't care about a degree. A few seemed to be impressed, but the majority were more apathetic. I think they realized at the time that they were making significantly more than I was—due to the overtime afforded the more senior people—and they had no student loans to pay back! That position brings with it a certain comfort. In addition, the Union guys opened my eyes to a lot of the world—pointing out both good and bad things about companies, the Union, the government, and the world, in general. Although I did not agree with all of their views, I am grateful for their sharing their insights. On to the lessons learned! You may recall that I mentioned my mentor at PepsiCo, Harry Delonge, earlier in this book. He taught me a lot, about people, about the company, and about the world of water treatment and chemistry. Most importantly, though, he taught me to teach myself—and in the end, we BOTH ended up a little smarter. This says a mouth full—about education, about imparting knowledge, and about collaboration. Many of the lessons learned in this chapter were, in some way, informed by my friendship with Harry.

Two other people at PepsiCo have been critical in teaching me lessons, which I hope to share with the reader in some form. One is the person who ended up being the best man at my wedding, Rob Busacca. Rob, from West Virgina (or, as he says, tongue-in-cheek, from "West by God Virgina"), joined the company a month after I did, soon after his mom passed away from a horrible battle with cancer. I was presumptuous enough to openly ask him about what he went through with his mom, and I think this candor—and sharing of personal experiences—from the very beginning is what helped cement the foundation of our friendship which remains strong to this day. Rob, like Harry, taught me many "life lessons." Rob also taught me more formally about business. After all, he read the Wall Street Journal from cover to cover every single day, at a point in time when I had never even opened one! I relied on him to deliver the condensed version of what was happening in the business world, and he did a great job. Rob later left the Union and became my manager, and I am thrilled to say that our friendship never once—not for a second—impacted our professional reporting relationship, which says a lot about Rob as a person. He taught me integrity in the workplace, balance, candor, and so much more.

The other person at PepsiCo who started a couple of years after I did, and who remains with me at PepsiCo as an undyingly loyal and trusted compatriot, is Lynda Costa. Unlike Rob and Harry, Lynda didn't specifically teach me about business, but she did teach me about people, and how to interact with them. She taught by her own example how successful we can be in business—and in life—if we treat each other with compassion, honesty, courtesy, and—simply—as we would like to be treated ourselves. I swear the stories about Harry, Rob, Lynda, and the cast of so many characters that have passed through the doors at PepsiCo are those of which movies are made, but that is for another book—or maybe for the big screen.

The lessons follow, really in no particular order of either chronology or importance; they are being captured here in Rhode Island as a sort of stream of consciousness as I contemplate them with the sounds of the ocean surf in the background.

Lesson 1: "Make people part of the process."

Earlier in this book, I mentioned a couple of lessons that I learned from Harry. The story that I told briefly in chapter seven provided lessons so valuable to me that I believe it is worth recounting in greater detail here. The story goes back to the days before email, and even before faxes...when there was this prehistoric monster called a TELEX—kind of like a telegraph, I suppose. This was really the most dependable way with which to communicate to our international operations people in many different time zones. Virtually all of our offices abroad had TELEX machines, and this is precisely the way that we in the Support Center (called the Headquarters back then) would receive requests for assistance from our employees around the world.

As Harry was training me in water treatment and chemistry, we evolved to the point where we would receive a request for help from, for example, someone in Saudi Arabia at one of our plants, and Harry would allow me to take a shot at developing a technical reply. He would then review my reply before we responded to the Field requestor. When I received the request, being a type-A personality, I wanted to be sure that the response I provided was PERFECT—or as close to perfect as it could be. So, I would take the TELEX request, then go off for a few days or a week, collect technical information that I needed, obtain literature data, all the time working feverishly to pen what I thought was the most robust response I could muster. THEN, once I had this all ready, I would trouble over the perfect *wording* for the TELEX reply. Guess what I forgot? To communicate in the interim with the requestor!

Think about this poor guy somewhere in Saudi Arabia, probably with a water treatment system that stopped working, which means that the plant would have to stop production, which means that potentially our products could not make it to the store shelves...he reaches out to the experts in the New York headquarters, via TELEX (which is a challenge in and of itself)...and then hears nothing...for 24 hours, 48 hours, sometimes for even a week. Sure, once he received the response, it was great, but imagine the angst he was feeling for that time period! The simple solution? COMMUNICATE.

Harry quickly taught me that over-communicating is WAY better than under-communicating (and I have since learned, by the way, that this works VERY effectively in marriage and other relationships as well!). I quickly learned that when a TELEX came in, it was best to take a few seconds to respond—IMMEDIATELY—to the requestor, simply to let them know that I received the request, knew it was important to them, and was working on a response to provide as soon as possible. This little technique, which now seems like such common sense, had a HUGE impact. I became someone in the Support Center who was regarded by the people in the Field as someone who was available and responsive, and who could always be depended upon to help. A great lesson to heed.

Lesson 2: Sometimes, it's okay not to be "buttoned up."

Another "Harry-ism." This is part of the same Harry story above, but, again, this aspect of it deserves a bit more elaboration. This lesson is equally as critical to success as the first—particularly in the corporate world. Being "buttoned up" in this case means waiting as long as it takes to get all the information you need to be completely confident in a reply...all the proverbial "i" s are dotted and "t" s are crossed. It also usually means that the risk of being wrong is low, because you have been so diligent in crafting a reply.

Don't get me wrong, being confident is good, and being diligent is good. This lesson is more a lesson of degree. In academia, for example, PhD scientists working on a sensitive genetic manipulation which could, perhaps, result in a cure for pancreatic cancer, would require a darned high level of diligence in what they are doing. Would a landscaper digging a hole in the ground to plant a tree? Astroscientists from NASA, charged with bringing home astronauts who have just been on a lunar or interplanetary mission would certainly require supreme levels of accuracy and precision. Would the porter who mops the floors in a local museum? I'm sure you get the idea. Certain actions in business, and the decisions upon which they are based, do not require—nor are they afforded the time for this—that you be completely "buttoned up." Many examples exist of remarkable successes in the business world that were achieved because someone ACTED—stopped thinking about and analyzing things—and did something. They knew that the opportunities would disappear if they waited, so were willing to take the risk associated with not being completely "buttoned up," and it paid off.

As you move up in an organization, part of the evidence of executive maturity is precisely the ability to weigh the pros and cons of a situation, and make a decision...and make it quickly. This is something that is very difficult to teach, but the first step is recognizing that this is a very clear reality. If you can develop this ability, it is very valuable. This doesn't mean to make a decision just for the sake of making a decision. Nor does it mean "shooting from the hip," as they say, making reckless decisions because you did not think of asking the right questions or acquiring the necessary information when it did exist. Rather, the real value is in striking the right balance—risk vs. benefit vs. time.

Lesson 3. It's often better to be the driver holding the reigns than the stallion in the front pulling the coach.

This one requires a bit more explanation than the others, especially if this book is being translated into non-English languages. I have seen so many of my colleagues over the years who want to be the "stallion" in this metaphor--not particularly collaborative, not great in working with teams, and not particularly willing to share the work...but clearly wanting to get the credit and reap the rewards. Sometimes this works, but not often...and when it does work, it usually doesn't last; it's not a sustainable approach to things. On the other hand, imagine the person with the reigns. This is the real "leader," not the stallion who just happens to be in the lead position. The driver is charged with guiding the entire team of horses (including the overly-zealous stallion) to work together, to move in the right direction, to avoid any pitfalls in the road, to know when the team needs a rest and when to spur it onward, and to make sure that the coach, with the entire team and all of its contents, arrives at the intended destination. Now, that's influence...and leadership. Not much different than the characteristics that would be expected of a good corporate leader. Learn this approach and use it; it works!

Lesson 4: A career is like a ferris wheel, with ups and downs.

The main thing is that, if you are at a low point, you stay on the ride, because soon enough you will be back on top. This is another very important lesson to remember. Every career will, indeed, have its ups and downs. There are days when you feel like closing up shop at your current company and calling an executive recruiter to "keep your options open." I'm convinced that in almost all cases, this is less a legitimate intent to move to another company and more a psychologic technique to reaffirm your own value! If it works, makes you feel better, and helps you see that things aren't as bad as you thought, then the exercise was probably worth it!

When you're at a low point, know that things will almost always improve. There is no feeling like when you "ace" a meeting with a CEO or when your "perfect" e-mail receives rave reviews from your manager, or when you know that you did a great job with a presentation. Enjoy the feeling while it lasts, because it may not last too long! Realizing this and understanding that this is perfectly natural happens to everyone makes the high points more rewarding and the low points easier to endure.

Don't be a "yes man" or "yes woman". I know that it's difficult for people in the corporate sector, especially those who are more junior in position, new to a company, or just beginning their careers, to sometimes "push back" or disagree with their managers or with colleagues who are more senior in the organization. As difficult as it is, please understand that there are times when you must do it. In general, and of course there are exceptions, the more senior you are in a company, the more you WANT people to disagree with you, when it is done correctly. You definitely don't want to push back merely to be contrary, but if you see something about a position or a proposed strategy with which you do not agree, you owe it to the company and its leadership to courteously voice your opinion in a rational, data-based, logical manner.

Never compromise your integrity. I know this sounds

like the things of which management text books are made…or the things that you hear parents tell their children in those sappy movies. But it's true. At the end of the day, you have to be able to live with yourself. If you compromise your integrity, the things that are important to you, your foundational values, then you compromise your very being. It's just not worth it.

Lesson 7: Learn how to articulate your passion.

As part of my current role with PepsiCo, I have the great fortune of traveling to many places to tell the story of the really impactful things PepsiCo is doing across the world—in environment, nutrition, agriculture, and with our associates. In fact, our associates are known for their passion…our Chair and CEO calls it the "passion of PepsiCo people," with their "can do" spirit. It's very true…it is astounding how much passion I have witnessed across the world for various causes. This is especially true when I guest lecture to college and university audiences. It is heart-warming and inspiring to see these hundreds of young adults (I used to call them kids, but I thought that might come across as a little condescending, which is not the intent) and the passion that inspires them.

Passion for one's work, indeed, is one of the most important things a person can find in the workplace. I won't reiterate the story of finding my own passion, which I described at the beginning of the book, but just know that once you find it, it is transformative. Just as passion which is channeled, and which is allowed to flourish, is transformational, this same passion can prove to be an unparalleled source of frustration. Why? This usually happens when the person who has the passion cannot adequately articulate that passion. It doesn't lessen the magnitude of the passion you feel, just how your actions and approaches are perceived—and received—by others.

One quick example. I have three sisters, all older than I. For years, one of them has had an unwaveringly strong social conscience. The list of her causes seems to increase with each week, but she genuinely remains passionate about all of them. However, she is the perfect example of not knowing how—or not having the current capability— to articulate the subject of her passions. The result, sadly, is one which is common for many people who cannot effectively communicate the things about which they are so emphatic: frustration and exasperation. In my sister's case, she knows in her mind and her heart what is important to her, and for what she is fighting and advocating, but cannot effectively and impactfully communicate that to others. My counsel to her, provided with the deepest love one can have for a sibling, has been the same counsel I provide to you as a reader if you find yourself in a similar state—learn to articulate your passion. Do it emphatically, but not adversarially; do it passionately, but not over-zealously; and do it logically and rationally.

Lesson 8: Go with your "gut feeling."

Remember I said that these lessons are listed in no particular order of importance? Well, if I had to pick a single one that is THE most important piece of advice I could relate, it would be this one. And it comes from Rob, whom I mentioned earlier in this chapter. He was famous for asking, "what does your gut tell you?" It has proven to be accurate many times over the years for me, and for several of my colleagues across multiple industries. I don't think scientists have quite deciphered what, precisely, is responsible for this "gut feeling," but it is real, nonetheless. In my estimation, it is somehow your body's aggregation of many intangible sources of input—intellect, social mores, religious beliefs, morality, integrity, communal perception, and so much more. All of these somehow get translated into a single, unmistakable "feeling" in your "gut"—in the deep of your stomach. Let me say that again—UNMISTAKABLE. I am absolutely convinced that if you ask someone, "what does your gut tell you?" and they answer, "I don't know,"—then they are either in denial (because their gut is telling them something other than what their brain wants to do), or that they merely have not yet come in touch with what they need to do.

This is not to say that if you go with your gut feeling everything will continue to go well and you will never be presented with any difficult challenges or hardships. I will tell you, though, that if you DO make a habit of going with what your gut tells you, you will absolutely be better off in the long run...no matter what the decision, or what the topic. The "gut" doesn't lie, and isn't subject to the errors of logic or the failings of emotion. It's important that you know, however, it is not always easy to follow your gut feeling, nor is it sometimes without pain or tribulation.

Let me emphasize this with one real-life example that happened to someone very close to me, and which has nothing to do with the corporate world. A relative had been dating the same man for over 10 years...she was madly in love with him. Engagement followed, and the lead-up to the wedding was not without its arguments and disagreements, but nothing that anyone externally would consider evidence of a "deal breaker" to postpone or call off the wedding. On the day of the wedding—and we only learned this in retrospect—the groom had gone to the priest on the day of the wedding and told the priest that he felt he was making a mistake. The priest dismissed what was the groom-to-be's "gut feeling" as "normal misgivings for anyone about to be married." The groom also ignored his gut feeling, and decided to proceed with the wedding. After 10 years of dating, they were divorced in six months. Listen to your gut feeling, no matter how difficult it may be!

About the author

Dan Bena is currently the Director of Sustainable Development for PepsiCo, and was formerly the Director of Technical Insight and Communication, where he served as liaison between technical functions, government affairs, public policy, and field operations to develop key messaging to internal and external stakeholder groups. He is now helping to lead the company's international Sustainability efforts across their beverage and foods operations, serving consumers in nearly 200 countries. Dan serves as Chair of the Washington-based American Beverage Association's Water Resources Committee and has been an active participant in various ABA Task Forces. He has been active in the International Society of Beverage Technologists (ISBT), as demonstrated by his having served as past Secretary of the Computer Applications Committee and being founder and Chair of the Emerging Scientific Interests Subcommittee, and—most recently—founder and Co-chair of the Subcommittee for Sustainable Development. He recently completed a three-year elected term on the ISBT Board of Directors, and was presented with the ISBT "Best Paper" Award on two occasions, for papers addressing the environment and sustainable development.

Dan also serves on the Board-sponsored Public Health Committee of the Safe Water Network, which is a not-for-profit organization for which PepsiCo was a founding member, dedicated to providing sustainable community-level solutions to provide safe drinking water in developing economies. Bena is also on the Editorial Advisory Board of Food Safety Magazine, and has served as an Associate Referee for the International Commission on Uniform Methods in Sugar Analysis (ICUMSA), contributed monographs to the Food Chemicals Codex (FCC), and reviewed manuscripts for the Codex Alimentarius Commission (CODEX). Dan is also a member of the Water Core Working Group of the World Business Council for Sustainable Development (WBCSD), and served as reviewer and contributor to the *Agricultural Ecosystems: Facts and Trends* white paper from WBCSD. He also was a member of the Advisory Board for development of the WBCSD Water Resource Risk Tool, which was launched to great acclaim at Stockholm World Water Week in August of 2007. Bena also serves on the Water Planning Board and Water Global Agenda Council of the World Economic Forum and the Steering Committee of the United Nations CEO Water Mandate. In 2009, he was invited by the mayor of his city to serve on a new Sustainability Advisory Board. The city is one of only three nationwide selected to pilot a new sustainability planning tool kit.

Bena has spoken in many venues addressing Sustainable Development, including his recent opening keynote address for the World Brewing Congress in August, 2008; his presentation to the Corporate Water Footprinting Conference in San Francisco in December, 2008; and his keynote address to the Soap and Detergent Association in January, 2009. In April, 2009, he participated in a provocative panel at the World Bank's Executive Development Program, entitled *Inclusive Agribusiness: Fighting Poverty, Hunger, and Malnutrition*. Dan enjoys academic guest lecturing, most recently for a "Difficult Dialogs" series at Northwestern University Kellogg School and an Environmental Careers series at the Columbia University School of International Public Affairs. He has authored chapters for several texts from CRC, Blackwell Science, and Marcel Dekker in the areas of water treatment and chemistry, sanitation, and beverage production. He lives in New York with his wife of 24 years, Diane, and their Westie, Opie.

Dan is a passionate and impactful public speaker serving an eclectic variety of topics. 100% of his speaking honorarium is donated to a variety of non-profit organizations that are dedicated to helping the planet and the people who borrow from and depend on it.